HUMAN BEHAVIOR

Human Behavioral Psychology and the Best Techniques of Body Language. Learn the Mysteries behind the Words

By

Jake Bishops

Table of Contents

Introduction 6

Chapter 1: Body Language 7

    Lower Body 8

    Legs Touching 8

    Pointing Feet 9

    Smarty Pants 9

    Shy Tangle 10

    Upper Body 10

    Leaning 10

    The Superman 11

    The Chest in Profile 11

    Outward Thrust Chest 12

    Hands 12

    Control 13

    Greeting 13

        Dominance 14

        Affection 14

        Submission 14

Holding..15

Chapter 2: Thoughts and Actions 17

Link between Thoughts, Decisions, Actions, and Reality   17

Thoughts 18

Feelings 18

Behaviors 19

Chapter 3: The Role of Defense 31

The Steps to Raise Self-Esteem 31

Acceptance... 32

Increase Awareness.. 34

Detach with Love 36

Chapter 4: Toxic People 24

How Negative and Toxic People Affect Your Life ... 29

Managing Negative Thoughts................................... 29

Chapter 5: How to Fake Your Body Language 39

Concentrate on the Eyes - Eye Conduct Can Be Telling   39

Look at the Face - Body Language Touching Mouth or Smiling 40

Focus on Vicinity 40

Check Whether the Other Individual Is Reflecting You   41

Take a Quick Check at the Other Individual's Feet 42

Watch for Hand Signals 43

Look at the Situation of the Arms 44

A Wrinkled Brow Can Occur in a Brief Instant and Uncover Negative Feelings 45

Chapter 6: Effects of Narcissism in Relationships 48

Why Am I Attracting Narcissists? 50

Caregiving Spirit *51*

You Fall for the Name-Dropping Charm *51*

Flattery Is Your Undoing *52*

Hovering for a Second Chance *52*

You Sustain the Drama *53*

You Are a Hopeless Empath *54*

Why Empaths Attract Narcissists *55*

You Are a Natural Healer *56*

Chapter 7: Knowing the Woman's Mind 57

How Women Process Attraction 59

Chapter 8: Deception 63

The Types of Deception 64

Lies *66*

Equivocations *66*

Concealments *66*

Exaggerations 67

Understatements 67

Untruthful 67

Identity 68

Relational 68

Instrumental 68

Simulation 69

How to Use Deception 70

Chapter 9: Distance in Communication 71

Conclusion 78

© Copyright 2021 by Jake Bishops - All rights reserved.

Introduction

The way a person acts in his or her relationships with others, especially in response to social situations that require a standard of conduct under pre-established rules of living. Psychologists have defined behavior as the set of responses that can be observed in a living organism. Sociologically, the behavior is understood as the role played by the individual in meetings and acts of coexistence, following the rules that establish the moral sense, customs, and habits of a particular group.

Behavior is the way a person behaves in front of others or in front of disparate situations. Mutual respect, self-esteem, moderation, generosity, and the capacity or impossibility of giving and accepting affection are characteristics of behavior, which, to be correct, must be under customs, laws, and traditions.

Chapter 1: Body Language

Being able to communicate well is extremely important when wanting to succeed in the personal and professional world, but it isn't the words you say that scream. It is your body language that does the screaming. Your gestures, posture, eye contact, facial expressions, and tone of voice are your best communication tools. These can confuse, undermine, offend, build trust, draw others in, or put someone at ease.

There are many times where what someone says and what their body language says is different. Non-verbal communication could do five things:

- **Substitute** – It could be used in place of a verbal message.
- **Accent** – It could underline or accent your verbal message.
- **Complement** – It could complement or add to what you are saying verbally.
- **Repeat** – It could strengthen and repeat your verbal message.
- **Contradict** – It could go against what you are trying to say verbally to make your listener think that you are lying.

We are going to cover:

- **Gestures** – These have been woven into our lives. You might speak animatedly; argue with your hands, point, wave, or beckon. Gestures do change according to cultures.
- **Facial expressions** – You will learn that the face is expressive and able to show several emotions without speaking one word. Unlike what you say and other types of body language, facial expressions are usually universal.
- **Eye contact** – Because sight tends to be our strongest sense for most people, it is an important part of Non-verbal communication. The way someone looks at you could tell you whether they are attracted to you, affectionate, hostile, or interested. It might also help the conversation flow.
- **Body movement and posture** – Take a moment to think about how you view people based on how they hold their head, stand, walk around, and sit. The way a person carries gives you a lot of information. Non-verbal communication could go wrong in several different ways.

Lower Body

The arms share a lot of information. The hands share a lot more, but legs give us the exclamation point and can tell us exactly what someone is thinking. The legs could tell you if a person is open and comfortable. They could also who dominance or where they want to go.

Legs Touching

When a person is standing, they will only be able to touch their bottom or thighs. This can be done seductively or they could slap their legs as if they are saying "Let's go." It might also indicate irritation. This is when you have to pay attention to the context of the conversation. This is very important.

Pointing Feet

Look at the direction of a person's feet to see where their attention is. Their feet will always point toward what is on their mind or what they are concentrating on. Everyone has a lead foot, and it all depends on their dominant hand. If a person is talking that we are interested in is talking, our lead foot will be pointing toward them. But, if they want to leave the situation, you will notice their foot pointing toward an exit or the way they want to go. If a person is sitting during the conversation, look at where their feet are pointing to see what they are truly interested in.

Smarty Pants

This is a position where someone tries to make them look bigger. They will usually be seated with their legs splayed open and leaning back. They might even spread their arms out and lock them behind their head. This is normally used by people who feel dominant, superior, or confident.

Shy Tangle

This is usually something that women do more than men. Anyone who begins to feel shy or timid will sometimes entangle their legs by crossing them under and over to try to block out bad emotions and to make them look smaller. There is another shy leg twirl that people will do when they are standing. The actual act of this movement is crossing one leg over the other and hooking that foot behind their knee as if they are trying to scratch an itch.

Upper Body

Upper body language can show signs of defensiveness since the arms could easily be used as a shield. Upper body language could involve the chest. Let's look at some upper body language.

Leaning

If someone leans forward, it will move them closer to another person. There are two possible meanings to this. First, it will tell you that they are interested in something, which could just be what you are talking about. But this movement could also show romantic interest. Second, leaning forward could invade a person's personal space; hence, this shows them as a threat. This is often an aggressive display. This is done unconsciously by powerful people.

The Superman

Bodybuilders, models commonly use this, and it was made popular by Superman. This could have various meanings depending on how a person uses it. Within the animal world, animals will try to make themselves look bigger when they feel threatened. If you look at a house cat when they get spooked, they will stretch their legs and their fur stands on end. Humans also have this, even if it isn't as noticeable. This is why we get goosebumps. Because we can't make ourselves look bigger, we have to come up with arm gestures like putting our hands on our waist. This shows us that a person is getting ready to act assertively.

This is normal for athletes to do before a game or a wife who is nagging their spouse. A guy who is flirting with a girl will use this to look assertive. This is what we call a readiness gesture.

The Chest in Profile

If a person stands sideways or at a 45-degree angle, they are trying to accentuate their chest. They might also thrust out their chest, more on this in a minute. Women do this posture to show off their breasts, and men will do this to show off their profile.

Outward Thrust Chest

If someone pushes their chest out, they are trying to draw attention to this part of their body. This could also be used as a romantic display. Women understand that men have been programmed to be aroused by breasts. If you see a woman pushing her chest out, she might be inviting intimate relations. Men will thrust out their chest to show off their chest and possibly trying to hide their gut. The difference is that men will do this to women and other men.

Hands

Human hands have 27 bones and they are a very expressive part of the body. This gives us a lot of capability to handle our environment.

Reading palms isn't about just looking at the lines on the hands. After a person's face, the hands are the best source for body language. Hand gestures are different across cultures and one hand gesture might be innocent in one country but very offensive in another.

Hand signals may be small, but they show what our subconscious is thinking. A gesture might be exaggerated and done using both hands to show a point

Control

If a person is holding their hand with their palms facing down, they might be figuratively holding onto or restraining another person. This could be an authoritative action that is telling you to stop now. It might be a request asking you to calm down. This will be apparent if someone places their dominant hand on top of a handshake. If they are leaning on their desk with their palms flat, this shows dominance.

If their palms face outward toward another person, they might be trying to fend them off or push them away. They might be saying "stop, don't come closer."

If they are pointing their finger or their entire hand, they might be telling someone to leave now.

Greeting

Our hands are used a lot to greet other people. The most common way is with a handshake. Opening up the palm shows they don't have any weapons. This gets used when saluting, waving, or greeting others.

During this time, we get to touch another person and it might send various signals.

Dominance

It can be shown by shaking hands and placing the other hand on top. How long and how strong they shake the hand will tell you that they are deciding on when to stop the handshake.

Affection

It could be shown with the duration and speed of the handshake, smiles, and touching with the other hand. The similarity between this one and the dominant one could lead to a situation when a dominant person will try to pretend they are just being friendly.

Submission

It gets shown by placing their palms up. Floppy handshakes that are clammy along with a quick withdrawal also show submission.

Most handshakes use vertical palms that will show equality. They will be firm but won't crush and for the right amount of time so both parties know when they should let go.

Waving is a great way to greet people and could be performed from a long distance.

Salutes are normally done by the military, where a certain style is prescribed.

Holding

A person who has cupped hands shows they can hold something gently. They show delicacy or holding something fragile. Hands that grip will show desire, possessiveness, or ownership. The tighter the fist, the stronger they are feeling a specific emotion.

If someone is holding their own hands, they are trying to comfort themselves. They could be trying to restrain themselves so they will let somebody else talk. It could be used if they are angry and it is stopping them from attacking. If they are wringing their hands, they are feeling extremely nervous.

Holding their hands behind their back will show they are confident because they are opening up their front. They may hide their hands to conceal their tension. If one hand is gripping the other arm, the tighter and higher the grip, the tenser they are.

Two hands might show various desires. If one hand is forming a fist but the other is holding it back, this might show that they would like to punch somebody.

If someone is lying, they will try to control their hands. If they are holding them still, you might want to be a bit suspicious. Remember that these are just indicators and you should look for other signals.

If someone looks like they are holding onto an object like a pen or cup, this shows they are trying to comfort themselves. If a person is holding a cup but they are holding it very close and it looks like they are "hugging" the cup, they are hugging themselves. Holding onto any item with both hands shows they have closed themselves off from others.

Items might be used as a distraction to release nervous energy like holding a pen, but they are clicking it off and on, doodling, or messing with it. If their hands are clenched together in front of them but they are relaxed, and their thumbs are resting on each other, it might be showing pleasure.

Chapter 2: Thoughts and Actions

Link between Thoughts, Decisions, Actions, and Reality

There exists a strong link between your thoughts, decisions, actions, and reality. They form a never-ending cycle of reactions as your ideas influence your decision-making skills. Your choices shape the actions you take, and actions impact reality influencing thought patterns. So, it is safe to say that your thoughts also influence your reality. You will learn more about this interdependent relationship here.

There might have been times in your life where you look at a situation and wonder how you got there. At times, it could be something as simple as eating ice cream when you promised yourself you wouldn't. Other times, it could be a major decision with significant consequences, like impulsively quitting your job with no safety net. To understand how your thoughts truly affect your life, you need to understand their connection.

Thoughts

All the information around you is absorbed by the brain, which is then processed to form your thoughts. Your mind is essentially the gatekeeper of all the information present around you. It decides the relevance of this information and thereby decides which thoughts must get your mental focus. Thoughts can easily transform themselves into beliefs that influence our feelings. This influence can be negative as well as positive. Let us take the example of bingeing on ice cream. Perhaps the thought was simply, "I had a rough day, and I deserve something nice," or "I'm starving and this is my quickest option right now."

Feelings

Any emotional response to your thoughts or behaviors is known as a feeling. These act as indicators of your connection to a given situation. Feelings originate from past experiences as well as current perspectives. Things start getting a little tricky when you take a simple thought, "I am hungry," and add an emotional response to that thought. A lot of times we end up combining emotions from several other factors onto one specific thought, which really has nothing to do with that emotion. Thinking "I'm hungry," can have other connotations if linked to grief after receiving some bad news, stress from a hectic day, or anger from a fight.

Behaviors

The actions resulting from thoughts and feelings are known as behaviors. The way you behave is important because your thoughts are telling you that it is the best option at a given point. So, if you feel hungry, and feel stressed or sad, you might decide eating ice cream is the best way to deal with your emotions.

These three different aspects are interconnected, and one cannot exist without the other. So, when you start thinking about the impact your thoughts have, you will realize how much they affect your entire life. Thoughts not only trigger emotions but also guide your behavioral responses. Your perception of yourself and the world is altered by the way you feel. It, in turn, affects the way you respond to a given situation.

Your emotions and feelings guide your behavior, and your thoughts and beliefs guide your responses. You cannot act unless you have an idea on which you wish to initiate action and context as well. There's always a reason why we do the things that we do. Actions are never baseless, even if they seem completely random they are always caused by something even if you aren't aware of what. This something essentially relates to your feelings, emotions, thoughts, and beliefs. So, if you suddenly experience sadness, you might react in a specific way. If you feel angry or sad, your response will usually stem from your feelings at that moment. If you believe that someone should or should not do something, then your behavior might be triggered by your beliefs. For instance, if someone accidentally bumps into you, and you think they owe you an apology, and when they don't, your reaction if any will be triggered by your beliefs.

At times, you might be aware of any feelings or beliefs you have, and at times they are the result of underlying feelings you haven't processed yet. Feelings and beliefs don't appear out of thin air and have specific causes. They are generated from experience and starts from the moment you take your first breath until your last. Things will continue to happen, and we continue to come up with ideas about ourselves as well as the world around us. These experiences influence the way we feel about ourselves and the world.

For instance, a young child might be playing in the backyard, and after some time, decides to climb up a tree without success. Then, one day, he manages to scramble up the tree. He feels exuberant and triumphant in his success. He thinks it's the best time; he is having fun and feels safe. Then, suddenly, one of his parents comes out of the house and shouts at him for being in the tree. They tell him it's dangerous and he must never climb the tree again or will end up hurting himself. What is the child thinking at this moment?

He is young, unsure, and doesn't fully understand the world around him so it could be any of the following:

- Having fun or feelings of fun are not safe.
- The world outside is dangerous.
- My parents don't want me to have fun.
- They are unhappy when I am having fun.
- I am not necessarily safe, even when I think I am.
- I will hurt myself if I have fun.
- It is dangerous to do things alone.
- It is not a good idea to try anything new.
- My parents don't think I can do anything.

As time passes, the child might forget the decisions he made or the belief that was formed because of it. Although he won't always recall that memory, it will be lodged in his subconscious in some way. Any other event or experience that reinforces this belief will slowly form his attitude towards life. So, there might be a time when the child is having fun with his friends and starts feeling uncomfortable about a good situation he is in. He starts to withdraw, and the previous belief he has formed about fun is preventing him from having it now. He might not even remember why he feels this way, but he knows he doesn't like it. As he grows up, he might think that he's not supposed to trust himself or the decisions he makes. And all this is because of a simple misunderstanding. This example, as mentioned earlier, is an instance of how beliefs are formed and the way they influence decision-making, actions, and results.

Once you understand the relationship between your thought process and actions, you give yourself a chance to choose your reactions. It, in turn, allows you to change because you know you have a choice. You can work on understanding your feelings, become more conscious about your decisions, and take action. There are three important things you must keep in mind while understanding this relationship.

The first thing you must do is validate your feelings. Regardless of what it is, never ignore the way things make you feel. If you wish to change something about yourself, the first step is to acknowledge and accept. If you feel sad or depressed, don't allow anyone to tell you otherwise. It is okay to feel sad or depressed. As soon as you accept your feelings, it becomes easier to work on changing them. When you understand what you feel and why you feel, you can take corrective action.

The second step is to guide your thinking. There's one thing you can always control, and that is the way you think. Your brain merely absorbs information, but it is a conscious decision to form thoughts. You can control your thoughts, and it must never be the other way around. If you allow your thoughts to control you, your life will become chaotic.

The third step is action. You cannot hold yourself accountable for the way you feel or the way you think. However, you can and will always be held responsible for the way you act. Your behavior, performance, actions, and the results are all dependent on you. If you get angry at someone and lash out physically, you will be held accountable for any altercation. Once you understand what it means to be accountable, it becomes easier to take corrective action. By merely changing the way you look at a problem, you can come up with a wide range of solutions.

Chapter 3: Toxic People

You can identify toxic persons by their behavior. Some relationships are also found to be toxic. Toxic people are suffering deep within, and they cannot take care of their problems. The person cannot meet their needs and feelings. They suffer from these ungratified needs and desires. To ease the suffering, they are experiencing the persons, behave in outrageous ways and their lives are one huge dramatic comedy. They cover up their wounded nature by portraying themselves as martyrs, perfectionists, bullies, and victims of circumstances. They also try these behaviors as they seek to satisfy their needs and heal from the wounds they sustained earlier in their lives.

These persons are dramatic, and they thrive in environments filled its drama. The person enjoys the attention they get from acting out. As a result, the person will magnify the insignificant issues and overreact causing others to turn heads. With little to show off for in terms of personal achievements, the person feels irrelevant and invisible. Since the person wants to gain some recognition, they will seek drama in every situation to refocus others' attention. They are also needy, demanding attention all the time from everyone in their lives.

Toxic persons are also manipulative as they use other people to have their needs met. When you grow close to a toxic person, they will find ways to make you do things for them. They will fake illnesses to seek sympathy, which they use to benefit themselves. The person will act as a victim of his or her past. They will use their self-perceived wounds as an excuse for their outrageous behaviors and habits. The person is already aware of their weaknesses, and they do not want to lose your friendship along with its benefits, they will devise ways of manipulating you to stick close. They also enjoy controlling others to have them worshipping them and doing different tasks for them. Toxic people will enslave you by their demands and manipulative techniques, and if you are not aware of what is happening, you will lose yourself while trying to save them.

Toxic persons find faults in everything and everyone. They pass harsh judgment and criticism on themselves and others. The person cannot focus on positive things. They are also unable to expect positive outcomes. Even with such negative expectations, the person will not like the negative outcomes. They blame themselves and are too aware of their weaknesses. They will want to concentrate on their shortcomings and hardly see any significance in their strengths. The person fails to understand that no one is perfect, as we are all designed with weak points and strong points. When the person fails to recognize the strengths they hold, they are less likely to make an effort to discover their talents and unique abilities that are everyone's building blocks for success.

Toxic persons are also envious of others' achievements as they believe others are jealous of them too. They live in desperation, as they are always comparing themselves with others. The person lives in a moan-full mood as they compare other good fortunes with their misfortunes. It becomes difficult for such a person to see any beauty in their lives. The persons believe others are more advantaged, and they resent people who are doing better than them.

Toxic persons are more likely to hurt themselves because they do not find any value in their lives. The person has limited motivation, no goals, or plans for their future. These people also cause harm to others. They are at a higher risk of involving themselves in drugs. Such persons will hardly seek help as they don't view themselves as deserving of anyone's attention.

Toxic people are persistent in their demands, and however much you turn them down, they will persist. The person has no regard for the other person's values and personal principles. They are out to make others act out of their norm.

When having an interaction with a toxic person, your reaction to their words and behavior can lead to your acquiring toxicity. You need to watch your reactions and avoid losing your values to satisfy the person's demands. In such interactions don't lash out at the other person out of frustration, as it will result in drama in which you do not want to participate. You might also walk out on the other person once they start throwing negative remarks your way, which is an inferior way of facing challenges.

When in a relationship or friends with a toxic person, your life is chaotic in many ways:

You are in are always fixing the person's endless problems. Toxic people are attention seekers, and they will want to have others involved in sorting out their issues that seem to occur more often than normal. Some of the problems are of their creation as they attempt to have people around caring for them.

You are not comfortable with your own life and your progress in your goals. Friendship with toxic persons can ruin your life by diverting you from your personal purposes. The person demands all the attention they can get from you. If you are not cautious, you will set aside your goals and live to satisfy the person's demands. The negativity of the person can overcrowd your positivity, draining you out of your positive energy.

You feel exhausted following interaction with them. Toxic persons are tedious to deal with. Their constant demands will drain you physically and emotionally. You will listen to the person to complain about the least significant issues. Their views of others and life, in general, will haunt your intelligence.

Having them around fills you with anxiety. When you have a toxic person in your life; either family or close friend and you do not want to isolate from them, you have no choice but to tolerate them. You will experience anxiety when you are about to meet them because you would rather not. As you anticipate their behavior and attitude, you can't wait to get it over with.

You feel drained from their constant drama. Toxic people enjoy causing a scene as it draws others' attention. Whenever you are with the person; you are sure at some point they will over-react, causing others to focus their attention on you. If you are a nontoxic person, the experience will not be as thrilling. You will avoid interacting with the person, especially in a public setting because you do not want to be caught up in their drama.

When you are with the person, you feel as if you are getting out of touch with your being. You are either pushed around too much or reacting by controlling the toxic person. Toxic people have the habit of being too pushy. When you are driven to the edge by their persistence and demands you will result in acting too controlling to prevent them from pushing and dragging you around at their free will.

You also feel overly self-conscious and cautious. When in the company of toxic people, you can't predict what to expect from them. Their behaviors are rather shameful to an average person. You always feel like you are walking on glass.

How Negative and Toxic People Affect Your Life

Toxic and negative people are bound to infect you with their negative outlook on life. Their thoughts highly influence the behaviors of a person.

Interactions with others can also result in toxic relationships which are defined by the following;

Managing Negative Thoughts

Personal views and beliefs held by a person are a result of life-time experiences. Our beliefs are influenced by the environment we grew up in and other societal factors. Changing personal beliefs is a challenge because they make up our being. A person can't see any faults in their belief systems. Thought patterns are not easily notable either.

A person can manage negative thoughts in the following ways:

Start by consciously acknowledging the negative thoughts as they occur in your mind. When facing challenges, you will note your thought patterns shifting from solution seeking to self-defeating thoughts.

Once you have identified these negative thoughts, you can easily challenge them. Challenging our ideas involves trying to find enough evidence to support our conclusions. In challenging negative thoughts, we learn to introduce rational questioning in them. We look at the evidence in terms of the credibility of the source of this evidence; is the evidence we are basing our conclusion on credible? How trustworthy is the source of the information on which we are basing our conclusions? Are there facts supporting the evidence? Are these facts accurate? The answers to these questions will help us in passing judgment on the validity of our thoughts. Thoughts that are not substantiated enough should be discarded.

The following step involves replacing the negative thoughts with more positive ones. By embracing the positive thoughts and letting go of the negative, the person is effectively able to train the brain to focus on positivity. The challenging of negative thoughts might seem difficult to follow through, but over time it becomes natural for the person. People who have adopted the otherwise termed as Socrates questioning are always questioning the validity of their conclusions on decisions, and it helps them ineffective critical decision making.

Chapter 4: The Role of Defense

To avoid falling victim to manipulators, you have to build your defenses so that you are prepared for any manipulative strategies that they may try to use on you. The best way to build your defenses is by taking steps to improve your self-esteem and your willpower. However, as a point of caution, you should be very careful about how you build your defenses because you don't want to create restrictions that will keep you from living a fulfilled life.

For example, as you try to guard against manipulation, you can't act out of fear. You can't hide from the world just to avoid scenarios where someone might want to take advantage of you. Remember that the world is full of people with dark personality traits who may harbor malicious intentions, so acting out of fear won't protect you from anyone. In fact, it will just make you more of a target. As you build your defenses, make sure that start on the premise that you are willing to confront manipulators head-on, and you will never run away or recoil. If you act out of fear, you lose by default.

The Steps to Raise Self-Esteem

To help you build your defenses, we will discuss the eight steps that you have to take to raise your self-esteem and to increase your willpower by extension.

Acceptance

Acceptance is about assenting to the reality of a given situation. It's about recognizing that a certain condition or process is what it is, even if it's characterized by high levels of discomfort and negativity. It's about consciously submitting to the fact that something cannot be changed, and that its reality is not subject to interpretation. It's about making peace with the situation that you are in.

Acceptance is the opposite of denial. Even the most rational among us tend to be in denial about lots of things in their lives, which are settled facts in the real sense. Denial can be a coping mechanism, one that can keep us from being overwhelmed by the reality of a given situation. However, denial does us more harm than good, because unless we can accept something, we can't change it, and we will be stuck looking for alternative interpretations and explanations for our prevailing circumstances.

Without acceptance, the door remains wide open for malicious people to exploit us. Take the example of a patient who is told that he/she is terminally ill. After seeking the opinions of several medical professionals and getting the same diagnosis, the patient is still left with the choice of either accepting or denying the situation. The one who accepts it will make peace and try to make the best out of what little time he has. The one who stays in denial will become susceptible to tricksters, who may offer "alternative cures," and he may end up losing all his savings paying such people so that in the end, he leaves his family with nothing. That is an extreme example, but it perfectly illustrates why acceptance is important in avoiding manipulation, even if the reality may seem too painful to accept.

The most crucial form of acceptance is self-acceptance. It refers to the state of being satisfied with yourself, the way you currently are. Most people have trouble accepting themselves as they are. We are all in a constant strive for self-improvement. We want to be more successful, to be wealthier, to be more attractive, or to be perceived more positively by others. Even the most accomplished among us have issues with self-acceptance.

In many ways, the desire to be a better version of yourself can be seen as a positive thing; it can help you study harder in school, work harder to earn a promotion at work or exercise more to get in shape. However, the problem is there is always room for improvement, so no matter how high you ascend, the dissatisfaction will always be there, and it will make you vulnerable to manipulation by people who want to take advantage of your desires.

To defend against manipulation, you have to accept your reality, and you have to accept yourself. People tend to think that if they accept themselves, they won't try to improve—that couldn't be further from the truth. Accepting yourself means owning up to your flaws, and that gives you control over your life. With self-acceptance, attempts at self-improvement would come from within, so when you decide to change, you will be doing it for yourself and not for anyone else.

Increase Awareness

Increasing your awareness means having a higher level of alertness when it comes to understanding what's going on in your environment. It means paying close attention to your surroundings, and to the way people behave around you. The higher your level of awareness, the better you will be when it comes to adapting to your surroundings and understanding the motivations of the people you interact with.

When you become more aware, you will be able to catch on quickly when people try to manipulate you. Many of us tend to be preoccupied with our own thoughts that we hardly ever notice the cues of the people we interact with. We tend to live life on autopilot, so when other people try to seize control over our lives, we only notice it when it's too late. If you increase your awareness, you will be equipped with the skills necessary to identify all the red flags, and you will be able to stop most manipulators on their tracks before they can do any real harm.

The first step towards increasing your awareness is to learn about the tendencies of manipulative people. You now know enough to be able to spot people with ill motives, but you should understand that the worst kinds of manipulators are very good at concealing their motives, so you have to keep working on increasing your awareness.

To be truly aware of manipulative people, you have to approach all interactions with some levels of skepticism. We are not telling you to turn into a paranoid person who doesn't let anyone in; we are just saying that you should take a deeper look at each person you interact with. Try to study their body language and their words, and try to see if they are trying to hide something.

Apart from increasing your awareness, you have to increase your self-awareness as well. Many people confuse those two things, but they are entirely different concepts. Self-awareness is about understanding yourself. It's about having a clear concept of your own personality. You have to examine yourself and figure out what your strengths and weaknesses are, what your values and motivations are, and what kind of thoughts and emotions you are likely to have in specific situations. Self-awareness helps you understand both who you are and how other people perceive you.

Self-awareness works as a defense against manipulation because when you know who you truly are, it becomes more difficult for someone to alter your thoughts and perceptions. If you have strong and well-articulated values, it becomes harder for a manipulator to get you to abandon those values. People who like self-awareness are more likely to be gaslighted or to be subjected to other forms of mind control.

If you end up in a relationship with a manipulative person, self-awareness can help you keep your identity. Manipulators will try to tell you what to think and how to behave, but if you are self-aware, you will experience cognitive dissonance, and your brain will push back against any attempts at manipulation.

Detach with Love

Detaching with love is a defense against manipulation that is most commonly used by people who have loved ones who suffer from substance abuse problems. Even though it was conceptualized to help people deal with addicts, it can also work when you are dealing with manipulators.

Detaching with love is about showing love and compassion for others without taking responsibility for their actions. For example, if you have a family member who is a drug addict, the way it works is that you try to support them and encourage them to get clean, but you let them make their own decisions, and you let them suffer the consequences of their actions. If the addict doesn't come home, you don't waste your time looking for them in the seedy parts of the city, you stay at home, and you do the things that benefit you and make you happy.

The point of detaching with love is to stop trying to control other people's lives, even if you are doing it for their own good. The idea is that you accept that people are different from you and that they have their own free will.

Detaching from love can defend you from manipulation in many ways. Some manipulators want to exploit you by making you responsible for them. They want you to give them all your attention; that is how they control you.

When you detach with love, you will learn to stop fixing everyone's problems. So, when the manipulator tries to play the victim to gain your sympathy, you will keep doing whatever is in your best interest, and you will tell him or her to take responsibility for his or her own actions.

Some manipulators may take up self-destructive habits because they want to dominate you by making you clean up after them. When they do this, you can detach with love by letting them follow the paths they have taken, no matter where they lead them. If they are causing you harm, you can get away from them, but leave your door open. If they find the right path in the future and regain control over their own lives, you can let them in again. You have to make it very clear, through your words and actions that you will let them direct their own lives, and you won't take any responsibility for them.

Detaching with love is about accepting others for who they are and respecting them enough to let them be in charge of changing their own lives. When you feel responsible for someone, and he makes a choice that harms you both, oftentimes, you will react with fear, anger, or anxiety. To detach with love, you have to learn to let go of those negative emotions.

Manipulators count on the fact that you will react in a predictable way to their machinations, but when you detach with love, you learn to calm yourself down and think about your role in the other person's life before you take any sort of action. This will keep you from falling into the traps that manipulators will set for you.

Detaching with love builds your self-esteem because it allows you to put your own needs ahead of those of the people that try to manipulate you.

Chapter 5: How to Fake Your Body Language

Regardless of being in the workplace or out with our partners, the non-verbal communication of the people around us says a lot. Peruse the full article to gain proficiency with every one of the eight regular non-verbal communication signals.

Concentrate on the Eyes - Eye Conduct Can Be Telling

Powerlessness to look can demonstrate fatigue, lack of engagement, or even misdirection—particularly when somebody turns away and to the side. If an individual looks down, then again, it regularly shows anxiety or accommodation. Students expand when subjective exertion increments, so if somebody is centered on a person or thing they like, their understudies will consequently widen.

Understudy enlargement can be hard to recognize; however, under the correct conditions, you ought to have the option to spot it. Now and again, the expanded flickering rate demonstrates lying—particularly when joined by contacting the face (especially the mouth and eyes). Looking at something can recommend a longing for that thing. For instance, if somebody looks at the entryway, this may demonstrate a craving to leave.

Looking at an individual can show a longing to converse with the person in question. Regarding eye conduct, it is likewise proposed that looking upwards and to one side during discussion shows an untruth has been told while looking upwards and to one side demonstrates the individual is coming clean. The purpose behind this is individuals turn upward and to one side when utilizing their creative mind to come up with a story, and gaze upward and to one side when they are reviewing a genuine memory.

Look at the Face - Body Language Touching Mouth or Smiling

Give specific consideration to the mouth when attempting to disentangle non-verbal conduct.

An authentic grin recommends that the individual is glad and getting a charge out of the organization of the individuals around the person in question.

You may likewise see a slight scowl that endures not exactly a second before somebody grins. Tight, pressed together lips likewise show disappointment, while a casual mouth demonstrates a casual demeanor and positive temperament. Covering the mouth or contacting the lips with the hands or fingers when talking might be a pointer of lying.

Focus on Vicinity

The vicinity is the separation between you and the other individual. Focus on how close somebody stands or sits alongside you to decide whether they see you positively. Standing or sitting in closeness to somebody is maybe probably the best marker of affinity. You can enlighten a great deal regarding the sort of relationship two individuals have simply by watching the closeness between them.

Check Whether the Other Individual Is Reflecting You

Reflecting includes mirroring the other individual's non-verbal communication. When interfacing with somebody, verify whether the individual mirrors your conduct. For instance, if you are sitting at a table with somebody and lay an elbow on the table, hold up 10 seconds to check whether the other individual does likewise. Another basic reflecting motion includes tasting a beverage simultaneously. If somebody copies your non-verbal communication, this is a generally excellent sign that the person is attempting to build up compatibility with you. Take a stab at changing your body stance and check whether the other individual changes theirs correspondingly. Watch the head development

The speed at which an individual gestures their head when you are talking demonstrates their understanding—or absence of. Slow gesturing demonstrates that the individual is keen on what you are stating and needs you to keep talking. Quick gesturing demonstrates the individual has heard enough and needs you to complete the process of talking or give that person ago to talk. Tilting the head sideways during the discussion can be an indication of enthusiasm for what the other individual is stating. Tilting the head in reverse can be an indication of doubt or vulnerability. Individuals likewise point with the head or face at individuals they are keen on or share a partiality with. In gatherings and gatherings, you can tell who the individuals with power depend on how regularly individuals take a gander at them. Then again, the less-critical individuals are taken a gander at less frequently.

Take a Quick Check at the Other Individual's Feet

A piece of the body where individuals regularly "release" significant non-verbal signals is the feet. The reason individuals unexpectedly convey non-verbal messages through their feet is that they are generally so centered around controlling their outward appearances and chest area, situating that significant pieces of information are uncovered using the feet. When standing or sitting, an individual will, for the most part, point their feet toward the path they need to go. So and when you see that somebody's feet are pointed toward you, this can be a decent sign that they have a positive assessment of you.

This applies to one-on-one collaboration and gathering association. You can enlighten a ton regarding bunch elements just by contemplating the non-verbal communication of individuals included, especially what direction their feet are pointing. What's more, and when somebody has all the earmarks of being occupied with discussion with you, yet their feet are pointing toward another person, it's presumable the person would prefer to converse with that individual (in any case if the chest area signals recommend something else).

Watch for Hand Signals

Like the feet, the hands release significant non-verbal signals when looking at non-verbal communication. This is a significant hint when perusing non-verbal communication, so give close consideration to this. Watch non-verbal communication turns in pockets when standing. Search for specific hand signals, for example, the other individual placing their hands in their pockets or hand on head. This can show anything from apprehension to inside and out duplicity. Oblivious pointing demonstrated by hand motions can likewise say a lot.

When making hand signals, an individual will point in the general heading of the individual they share a partiality with (this non-verbal prompt is particularly essential to look for during gatherings and when connecting in gatherings). Supporting the head with the hand by laying an elbow on the table can demonstrate that the individual is tuning in and is keeping the head still to center. Supporting the head with the two elbows on the table, then again, can show weariness.

At the point when an individual holds an article between the person in question and the individual they are associated with, this fills in as an obstruction that is intended to shut out the other individual. For instance, if two individuals are talking, and one individual holds a stack of paper before that person, this is viewed as a blocking demonstration in non-verbal correspondence.

Look at the Situation of the Arms

Think about an individual's arms as the entryway to the body and oneself. If an individual folds their arms while interfacing with you, it is generally observed as a protective, blocking motion. Crossed arms can likewise show nervousness, powerlessness, or a shut personality. Whenever crossed arms are joined by a veritable grin and by and large loosened up stance, at that point, it can demonstrate a sure, loosened up frame of mind. When somebody puts their hands on their hips, it is normally used to apply predominance and is utilized by men more regularly than ladies.

Is non-verbal communication a "learnable aptitude," and can it in this manner be faked? The appropriate response is yes and no. Most by far of the more common non-verbal communication can be scholarly. For instance, keeping your hands out of your pockets or utilizing the hands expressively to stay legitimate and open, or repelling the hands from the face to appear to be increasingly certain as effectively learned through cognizant idea and redundancy. In any case, another zone of study uncovers that there is an entirely different arrangement of signs that are significantly harder to control, if certainly feasible.

A Wrinkled Brow Can Occur in a Brief Instant and Uncover Negative Feelings

These are called micro-expressions or micro-signals. These signs can be utilized to disentangle liars from truth-tellers. Micro-expressions show up as wrinkles, grins, glares, grins, and wrinkles and can offer a precise, however short-lived, window into feelings. These micro-expressions are constrained by muscles, for example, the frontalis, corrugator, and risorius, and they are incited by hidden feelings that are difficult to control deliberately. One of these feelings is the phony grin to demonstrate submission instead of certifiable euphoria or joy. The phony grin is self-evident because the lips are pulled over the mouth, yet the muscles controlling the eyes have no influence.

With particular PC programming, specialists have had the option to identify these signs. PCs were utilized because the sign moves quickly over the face in divisions of seconds, making it difficult for people to lift the sign deliberately.

Hindering video on rapid camcorders and playing it back over and over to spectators can likewise be utilized to distinguish the articulations. So some portion of the story is that micro-expressions are hard to recognize and control, yet the remainder of the story discloses to us that if they exist (and they do), that we should at some level have advanced the capacity to peruse and distinguish them. Along these lines, we should be mindful about accepting that since they happen so quickly, that they can't be gotten and on the other hand that we can without much of a stretch phony our way through the non-verbal channel. It could be that the subliminal instinct is working diligently, giving us that intuition feeling that can't confide in somebody despite not exactly having the option to put it to words. The reason, it appears, is a blend of micro-expressions and our instinct.

A few scientists will disclose to us that the face is the most straightforward piece of our bodies to control, yet this isn't valid and is a sorry excuse for the full story. If our countenances were so effectively controlled, why have Botox medicines stop up our appearances with low-level poisons to eradicate wrinkles? Why not simply quit utilizing the muscles out and out and, in this way, abstain from experiencing facial wrinkles during the maturing procedure? The straightforward answer is that it's not the basic.

While our countenances are in certainty under an enormous part under our influence, we can't generally be centered around it, in case we do not have the option to concentrate on whatever else.

Not the least of which is controlling our discourse. Would you be able to envision what it resembles to build sentences freestyle while attempting to stay expressive and yet abstain from contracting "unseemly" facial muscles (whatever they may be)? When we talk or see, or do, our faces normally react to what is happening around us since they are firmly attached to our psyche and our feelings. It is circumstances and logical results relationship, or even a weapons contest, and it correctly because the face gives such an immense measure of data that we are so fixed on understanding it.

Different approaches to detect phony concerns incongruent non-verbal communication. That is, a language that is conflicting with either the words being communicated in and the non-verbal language that goes with it.

Chapter 6: Effects of Narcissism in Relationships

You know you shouldn't fall in love with a narcissist, but somehow, you find yourself entangled in a toxic relationship with one. How did you end up here? After all, narcissists love no one else above themselves. You are looking for someone to love and cherish you as much as you love and cherish them, yet you end up with someone incapable of loving you or even recognizing you beyond a glance.

Why do we fall in love with narcissists? What is it about them, or ourselves, that makes this supposedly impossible connection possible? Someone who is too engrossed in their ideology of themselves should fundamentally be unattractive, yet here we are.

We live in a world where fantasy has been glorified, and everyone keeps chasing after something unreal at some point. At the back of your mind, you know what you seek, or what is before you is superficial, a smokescreen, yet the allure of attaining the impossible is too strong, so you yield.

Take speed dating, for example. Many people have participated in one or more. How do you get to know someone by summarizing highlights of their life? Speed dating is one of the lamest things in as far as relationships are concerned, yet many people throng the venues in the hope that they can find someone to settle with.

In such a case, who is at fault? Is it the narcissist who presents their case as a well-to-do, accomplished, person of your dreams kind of partner, or the seeker who is impressed by, and accepts nothing short of what the narcissist says they are? However, speed dating is not our concern, but an attempt at highlighting how complicated relationships can be, especially in terms of needs assessment (Houser, Horan, & Furler, 2008).

Narcissists are desperate, not just for attention, but also for self-love. They need to convince themselves that they are good enough constantly. If they are good enough for themselves, they have to be good enough for you too. This is one of the reasons why rejection doesn't always work well for a narcissist. It is not easy for them to reconcile it in their minds that someone thinks and feels they are not good enough.

While narcissists are at fault for their grandiose perception of themselves, at times you have to look inwards to understand your role in some unfortunate events. For the record, this is not to blame the victim, but to help you see things from a different perspective. Narcissists might be held accountable for manipulating you into a relationship, but you can get out. You deserve to be happy, and you deserve a happy and healthy relationship. Earlier on we saw some of the defining characteristics and manipulative traits of narcissists. This helped us understand who they are, how to identify them, and why they behave the way they do. We will try to understand you, the victim, and how narcissism is perpetuated in your life.

Why Am I Attracting Narcissists?

Ever felt like you are a narcissist magnet? Somehow, you keep ending up in relationships with narcissists, and this is not just about personal relationships, but the whole spectrum, including professional relations. While you might worry about attracting narcissists, this is not the main problem. The real problem is that you are holding onto them.

Let's try an exercise. Answer the following questions about your interactions and relationships truthfully:

- Do you have defined boundaries about behavior and attitudes you can tolerate from your partner?
- Would you end a relationship because your partner is selfish and doesn't consider your needs?
- How do you handle an abusive relationship? Walk away or stay and hope your partner will change?
- Do you excuse ill behavior from your partner and make excuses for them?

These might seem like mundane things, but they form the platform upon which a narcissistic partner will get away with devaluing you and your opinion all the time.

Here are some reasons why you might find yourself in a relationship with a narcissist, an abusive relationship you struggle to get out of:

Caregiving Spirit

Caregiving is a good deed. You empathize with someone who lacks, and out of the kindness of your heart, you take care of them. Many high achievers in society are in relationships with narcissists, some without knowing it. As a high achiever, you know you can take care of yourself. As a result, you always turn down the chance for someone to take care of you. You offer to pay for meals and drinks all the time. There is nothing wrong with taking care of yourself. However, to compensate for this lack of vulnerability, it is easier for you to take care of others. In so doing, you end up attracting people who constantly need help.

You Fall for the Name-Dropping Charm

Everyone knows someone important. When it comes to celebrity stories, everyone has something that can light up a conversation. Whether it is true or another story, they heard from someone else; they tell their tales so vividly you can almost live in the moment through their words.

"Oh, you know Vettel too? He's such a nice person. He's friends with one of my buddies at work; we hang out from time to time."

If this kind of thing works for you, there is a good chance you will never see beyond a narcissist's name-dropping charm. Their stories and encounters are full of big names. It gets worse when they realize these appeals to you. They do this in a bid to conceal their insecurities about themselves and instead, lavish you with the idea of this glamorous life they live. Be warned, however, this charm is ingenuine. It is a ploy to seek and maintain attention. After all, who doesn't want to hear more about how to sneak into Buckingham Palace?

Flattery Is Your Undoing

Flattery can make you feel so good, but it doesn't last. At best, it can get you in a good mood. Narcissists crave attention. Nothing stands in their way when they want it. The use of flattery works for them because they can flatter you to get your attention, then immediately go on about them.

Flattery for a narcissist is not necessarily about needing compliments. In some cases, it is about paranoia, as the narcissist goes through their regular attention-seeking routine, and to boost their fragile ego.

Hovering for a Second Chance

If you are in a relationship with a narcissist and you break up with them, please let them go. Don't hold on, hoping that they might change and come back better. Narcissists love to hover around in the aftermath of a breakup. They had all your attention, which they don't enjoy anymore. This makes them feel helpless and abandoned, in which case the only alternative is to lure you back by any means necessary.

There are several tricks that they can use for this, including making a half-hearted apology, convincing you that they will not do what made you break up again, and so forth. Some will even send you photos of themselves looking sad. All this is to guilt you into taking them back.

Remember that you let them go because they disrespected you, and you felt that they cannot change. Such a person cannot change in a few days. They can, however, learn how to camouflage their real intent. Most people who take their narcissistic partners back usually suffer more pain and emotional trauma than they did earlier on.

You Sustain the Drama

Narcissists get bolder over time. They come at your boundaries, hoping you will cave and get softer with them. Your life with them is full of so much drama; you can't seem to catch a break. Netflix would be jealous of your life. Think about this for a moment: how peaceful is your life when your narcissist partner is out of town for work, or when they have traveled for some other reason?

When you are all alone, things are easy, smooth, peaceful, until they come back and all the upheaval starts. A narcissist will always leave you devoid of energy. All their demands will leave you worn, drained, and exhausted. All you ever do is provide for everything they need, from attention to affection. At the beginning of your relationship, this might feel okay, because perhaps you are trying to impress them or keep up with their energy. However, after a while, you realize you cannot keep up, and you are demoralized after an encounter with them.

You Are a Hopeless Empath

If there is one category that narcissists love and are surprisingly more drawn to it, it has to be empaths. Life can be very cruel and unfair. Why do such nice, loving, and caring people end up with partners who leave them more worn out than confidential documents having passed through a paper shredder?

The secret lies in your personality. As an empath, you are an understanding person. You believe that everyone deserves a chance. You see the good in everyone, even when you shouldn't. You believe that given time, you can turn a bad person into a good person. If you spend enough time with them, you can show them the goodness of their hearts, and make them change and embrace a new life (Stadler, 2017). This is where you go wrong, and open your life to toxicity.

Narcissists are wounded animals. As an empath, you want to take care of them. They know this better than you do. They know you are naturally inclined to try and fix them. When you meet, they will talk about how rough life has been for them in the past, perhaps in relationships, or their work, or anything else that draws your sympathy. While it is okay to be kind, you must be very careful about whom you show your kindness to.

Why Empaths Attract Narcissists

The attraction between an empath and a narcissist is one of those instinctive connections that just happen. You feel like you were meant to be together. You clicked the very first time you met, and it seems you have found the right person for you until you wake up from the bad dream that has been months or years of your life. What's unfortunate for most empaths is that they will often end up in another relationship with another narcissist.

Narcissist-empath relationships are very toxic. You are exposed to so much pain that people who were once close to you can barely recognize you. Narcissists and empaths share some attributes that are attractive to one another, which is one of the reasons why they always seem destined to meet one another.

For the empath, however, it is nothing but bad news. All your goodness will be misconstrued for weakness and exploited by a narcissistic partner. To understand why this relationship happens in the first place, here are some reasons why you are drawn together:

You Are a Natural Healer

A narcissist will always appeal to an empath because you have natural healer tendencies. There is something so nurturing about you. Everyone knows it and it shows. You are a natural healer because you are sensitive. You are sensitive to people's feelings and needs.

Chapter 7: Knowing the Woman's Mind

Were you ever itching to get into the mind of a woman and ask what she is thinking exactly? But most people are motivated by the same fundamental motivations, as you are about to learn. When you know what they are, you can communicate with nearly every woman.

Also, if you haven't realized it, women are different from us. It's like they're from a whole other world sometimes, and they speak a different language. But it's not so difficult to understand people, and it's just different. Essentially, you need to understand the two primary ways women think differently from us.

How women get their way does not influence others in the same way that men do. We can't. They can't. We are less vulnerable than we are physically, and that is why most people (and some women) believe that they can easily overcome a woman through bullying. If a woman wants to get her way, she has to use other tools. The most common is the manipulation of the emotions of people.

She is a grown woman, and her emotions are controlled by her. However, men are real suckers for drama because they think they take responsibility for the emotional states of a woman.

When you think about it, it's hilarious. A woman can overwhelm a man with drama, literally. And who can blame them for this? For a very long time, it was their only choice. Not only physically are they weaker, but they have disadvantaged of authority for thousands of years and are compelled to use further creative ways to show men's strength. And of course, you've noticed that they've made it a science.

Let's clarify something before we go on: there is nothing wrong with the use of drama or manipulating people to do it. All of us use manipulation to obtain what we want. Some people refer to it as inspiration or influence. But we never force the person to respond to us, in any case.

In fact, men are more likely than drama to use bullying to get what they want. So it doesn't make sense to hate women to use the scene to get what they want. Instead, we will use this information to increase your choices for enhancing your relationships with women.

And that's just beginning to understand this: you will never find a woman who is "free of drama." People are emotional because it's a way to get what they want, what you have to do as a man is to learn how to handle the drama and prevent women from using it to dominate you. And believe it or not, this is precisely what women want of a man.

How Women Process Attraction

If this last statement puzzles you, it will clear the confusion to understand how women attract. This starts with understanding the one thing about women that most men have totally backward: what women want in a man. First, if you ask women for dating advice, that's right now because you'll just make yourself crazy. You might have worked this one out already.

Have you ever wondered why women don't seem to know what they want from a man's relationship? They say that they want a nice man who is good at treating a lady and who loves his wife. A sensitive man who opens the door to them asks them how beautiful they are and how wonderful a friend they are.

Instead; however, we are madly in love with people who are unrefined, crazy, cocky, a little childish, and who you just look at and wonder: "How the hell is this guy doing for him?" You are, in the meantime, the good-natured man who knows how to treat a lady and who loves his wife. A guy who is compassionate and caring and opens her door tells her how beautiful and kind she is.

And where do you get that? She slowly writes you out of her life as either a "great friend" or worse.

What's that all about in the world? You were the guy she said she needed. Why did you get to the place of your wife after watching her fall over her head for that "other jerk??" That's because what the women want is not what they think they want. And the sooner you recognize this, the sooner you will quit trapped in the' Friends' Corridor.' Now you shouldn't be shocked. After all, almost everyone does not claim that they want things that are entirely different from what their behavior reflects?

How many (men and women) do you know who is healthy, but who is consuming sugar-filled sweets, unhealthy fats, salt, and preservatives? How many people do you know who are wealthy, but who spend their money carelessly and who can't wait to go home to see TV throughout the day? This is because, while people want to be wealthy and safe, they are motivated by deeper motivations that most people don't take time to comprehend.

Don't tell people to judge. Many people are quite naive about the real reasons behind their actions, so they genuinely believe themselves when they tell you what they want. Yet look at their actions, if you want to know the real story.

Don't listen to what she says, if you want to know what women find attractive to look at her actions. Believe it or not, there's something "jerk" that most women like a flame moth.

They're making women feel safe and exciting.

This is an enticing mix because security and anticipation are two of the primary emotional needs people are looking for in romantic relations. If a man meets those two emotional requirements of a woman, he ignites a powerful unconscious attraction that transcends the reasoning mind of a woman.

Sound difficult to believe? Only think of how men you know who have given up thinking because of a woman's physical appeal. Think of how many people give up their thought and eat food they consider to be bad because they taste good. Think of how many people know who is spending their money on things which they don't need and end up having broken and then buy lottery tickets as "they want to be rich." This is why "jerks" (we will call them Bad boys) spark unconscious causes of attraction that seem to contradict a woman's spoken desires.

How's that?

First, these "bad boys" are immune to drama control, making them unpredictable... which are exciting for women.

Think about that, how exciting is it to a woman when a man answers her with what he wants because he is afraid to make her feel sad, frustrated, jealous, angry, unsure, stupid, or some other dramatic emotional state?

It's pretty dull, as you can imagine. The more beautiful a woman is, the more acquainted she is with people who bow to her every time she uses drama to dominate them. And frankly, she's all right with most people because it gives her more power. She just doesn't date such men.

She dates the people who can take over and who are not frightened by the drama. And that's where security and security are needed.

Think of this: how comfortable does a woman feel when she has a partner she can present? Does that mean he is insecure, weak, and obedient or reliable and trustworthy? Obviously, many women would like to have a nice man who knows how to treat the lady and who loves his wife. A caring, responsible man who opens her door tells her how beautiful and a great friend she is.

But most men are either: the nice man they say women want or the unrefined bad boy. Exceptionally few people could be both, and as the bad boy sees her need for security and excitement, she selects him above the boring man of beauty.

Chapter 8: Deception

Deception is going to refer to the act, whether it is kind or cruel or big or small, or causing someone to believe that something else is untrue. Even those who consider themselves pretty honest are going to practice some of this deception, and there are several studies out there that show how the average person, no matter how good-hearted they think they are, are going to lie several times in a day.

When it comes to these lies, some of them are going to be big lies that are meant to cause harm and hide the bad that the liar has done. But for the most part, the lies that we say are going to be small, usually white lies, that are used to spare the feelings of another person or get us out of a situation that is making us uncomfortable.

You will find that deception is not always going to be an act that is outward. It is also true that people are going to tell lies to them. There are a lot of reasons that they would do this, such as trying to maintain a healthy dose of self-esteem to some serious delusions that are sometimes beyond their control. While it is sometimes seen as harmful to lie even to yourself, some experts are likely to argue that certain types could also have a positive effect on your overall well-being as well.

Researchers have long searched for ways to find out when they can tell whether someone is lying or not. The polygraph test, which is something that a lot of us already know about, has long been controversial, and it has long been known that some people are easily able to lie to the test and get away with it. This is especially true if the individual has some psychiatric disorder.

With this, we need to take a look at why people lie. No one likes to feel deceived about anything, and when anyone, especially a public figure, ends up being caught in a lie, it can turn into a big headache for them. But while a lot of us are going to pride ourselves on our scrupulous honesty, and we try to stay as far away as possible from those who are fine with falsehoods, the truth is that all of us have lied at one point or another.

Experts find that having a small amount of deception can be important when it comes to maintaining a society that is healthy and can function well. The formal study of deception was once the domain of theologians and ethicists, but in recent years, more psychologists have turned over to look at the reasons why people are going to lie, as well as some of the conditions that make people more likely to lie.

The Types of Deception

Deception is going to include a lot of different things, but often, it is going to include a type of communication or omission that will serve to omit or change up the whole truth from another person. This is done in a manner that benefits the deceiver. If they hide the truth or change up the facts a little bit, then their victim will believe what the deceiver wants, and the deceiver will win. This can sometimes be a little white lie that helps to protect the feelings of the victim, but more often than not, it is going to be done at the expense of the victim.

Examples of this kind of deception are going to range from false statements to claims that are misleading, where relevant information is taken out. This is done so that the victim is going to be led to a false conclusion. In some cases, we may think that this oil is going to benefit the health of our brain more than some other foods we would eat.

However, the amount of omega-3 fatty acids that are found in sunflower oil is going to be low. And thanks to the other ingredients found in the oil, it is usually not seen as something that is all that good for the health of your brain. So, while sunflower oil does have some omega-3 fatty acids, and those are good for your brain, the information is going to lead the victim to infer false information about just how beneficial the sunflower oil is for them.

When it comes to deception, we have to look at the intent of the deceiver. If they got the information wrong on accident and shared it with the victim, then this is not deception. But if the deceiver wants to make sure that the victim is getting the wrong information on purpose, then it is going to be deception. The intent is going to be vital because it is going to show us the difference between an honest mistake and deception.

A good thing to look at here is the Interpersonal Deception Theory. This theory is going to explore some of the interrelations that show up between the communicative context and the sender and receiver cognitions and the behaviors in the exchange.

Now, there are going to be a few different types of deception that can show up depending on the situation and what the deceiver is hoping to get out of the exchange. Some of the forms of deception that you can use or encounter in your life include:

Lies

This is when you will make up information or when the deceiver is going to give information that is opposite of the truth, or at least very different from the truth.

Equivocations

This is when the deceiver is going to make a contradictory, ambiguous, or indirect statement.

Concealments

This is when the deceiver is going to omit some important information or relevant to the given context, or they are going to engage in some behavior that will ensure that the relevant information is as hidden as possible.

Exaggerations

This is when there is a big overstatement, or the deceiver is going to stretch the truth as much as they can get away with.

Understatements

This one is going to head in the opposite direction. With this one, you are going to find that the deceiver is going to downplay the aspects of the truth as much as possible.

Untruthful

This is also going to be when the deceiver is going to try and misinterpret the truth a bit.

Many of us think that we are good at deception. However, this takes a lot of talent and work, and since most people are good at catching lies and deception, it is hard to pull off on someone.

Three main motives are focused often on when it comes to why people like to lie and deceive others. According to Buller and Burgoon (1996), there are three methods that you can use to distinguish deception based on that interpersonal deception theory from before. These include:

Identity

The deceiver may lie to save their self-image or to remain in the same position with others, or with that one person, as they did before.

Relational

This is the deception that is done to help maintain the bonds or the relationships that you have.

Instrumental

This is when the deceiver is going to lie because it helps them to protect their resources or avoid any punishment that they should receive.

Depending on who uses the deception, it can sometimes be easy to see. Many of us think that we are good at deceiving those around us when, in reality, we are not. We end up being caught, especially if we are close to the other person we are trying to deceive.

But some people are good at deceiving. They are so good at this that they can end up deceiving someone for many years or more, and the victim, as well as those around them sometimes, will never be any the wiser about it. This can be dangerous because often, we don't know what is being kept from us and what we should know about a particular situation.

Simulation

Simulation is going to be any time that the deceiver exhibits some false information. There are going to be three different techniques that can be used with this, including mimicry, fabrication, and distraction. Let's dive into each of these to see how they work.

The first method is mimicry. This is when you will copy another example or another model. For example, animals are going to use this to deceive their predators through auditory or visual means in most cases.

Then there is the idea of fabrication. This is when the other person is going to make up a brand-new lie or story that fits their needs. For the deceiver to make something appear to be something that it isn't, usually to encourage the other person to divert, endanger, or reveal the victim's resources, is going to be a fabrication. The deceiver wants to learn something from the other person, and they want to cause some harm to the victim. This means that they are going to tell a fabrication to completely throw the victim off guard and make it so that they aren't sure what to believe.

An excellent example of this would occur in World War II. During this time, it was common for the Allies to work with hollow tanks that they would make out of wood rather than the usual materials. This was done so that the German planes would think that a large unit of them was moving in on an area. In reality, the real tanks were hidden and were moving in the opposite direction towards their real target.

Distraction is the next simulation. This is when the manipulator is going to try and get someone's attention from the truth, usually with some bait, or something that they know will divert the attention away from whatever the deceiver is trying to hide. Bait and switch, as well as many of the fraud techniques that we hear about, are going to work with the idea of distraction as well.

How to Use Deception

Now that we have a better idea of what deception is all about, it is time to look at a few of the techniques that you can use to put deception to work for your own needs. It is often not considered ethical to use deception, even though most people are going to use it at one point or another to get what they want. Learning how to use deception properly can make it more likely that someone is going to do what you want.

Chapter 9: Distance in Communication

Focusing on the United States, there are four types of distances that people use to communicate on a face-to-face basis. These distances are intimate, personal distance, social distance, and public distance. Starting with the intimate distance, it is used for highly confidential exchanges as zero to two feet of space between two individuals marks this zone. An example of intimate distance includes two people hugging, standing side-by-side, or holding hands. Individuals with intimate distance share a unique level of comfort with one another. If one is not comfortable with someone approaching them in the intimate zone, he/she will experience a significant deal of social discomfort.

Firstly, personal distance is used for talking with family as well as close acquaintances. The personal distance can range from two to four feet. Akin to intimate distance, if a stranger walks into the personal zone, the one is likely to feel uneasy being in such proximity with the stranger.

Secondly, there is the social distance used in business exchanges or when meeting new people and interacting with groups of people. Compared to the other distances, social distance has a larger range in the range that it can incorporate. Its range is four to twelve feet, and it depends on the context. It is used among students, acquaintances, or co-workers. As expected, most participants in the social distance do not show physical contact with one another. Generally, people are likely to be very specific concerning the degree of social distance that is preferred, as some require more physical distance compared to others. In most cases, the individual will adjust backward or forward to get the appropriate social distance necessary for social interactions.

Thirdly, we have public distance, which is twelve or more feet between individuals. An example of public distance is where two people sit on a bench in a public park. In most cases, the two people on a bench in a public park will sit at the farthest ends of each other to preserve the public space. Each of the earlier types of proximity will significantly influence an individual's perception of what is the appropriate type of distance in specific contexts. One of the factors that contribute to individual perceptions of how proxemics should be used is culture. Individuals from different cultures show different viewpoints on what the appropriate persona; space should be.

Fourthly, there is the concept of territoriality, where individuals tend to feel like they own and should control their personal areas. We are inclined to defend our personal space. When someone invades this personal space, then the individual will react negatively as it is an invasion of territory without express permission. At one point, you asked a stranger to keep some distance from you because you felt uncomfortable with the person standing close to you. Sometimes standing next to a person may also denote that you are creepy and may be intending to harm the person.

If one is talking to someone, the person violates your personal space, and you allow it, then it signals that you are okay to intimate ideas. Intimate ideas in this context include highly personal issues that one can talk about with another person. For instance, if you walk and sit close and in contact with a woman watching television and she approves of your behavior, then it is indicative that she is likely to allow you to have a personal talk that may be intimate in nature. Such discussion may include your health challenges or mental health and not necessarily sexual issues. For this reason, one should carefully weigh the need to invade the personal distance.

Regarding children, violating personal distance will make them freeze due to feeling uncomfortable. If a teacher sits next to a student or stands next to a student, then the student is likely to feel uneasy and nervous. However, they are instances where the invasion of personal space is allowed and seen as necessary. For instance, during interviews or when being examined by a doctor, invasion of private space by the person with an advantage is allowed. The panel during an interview may move or ask you to move closer, which may violate your personal space. A doctor may also stand closer to you, invading your personal space, but this is necessary due to the professional demand for their service.

As such, when one avoids personal distance, and the individual is expected to be within this space, then the individual may be feeling less confident or feeling ashamed. For instance, if a child has done something embarrassing, he or she is likely to sit or stand far from the parent during a conversation. For this reason, it appears that one should feel confident, assured, and appreciated to approach and remain in personal space when needed.

Additionally, staying in personal space during intense emotions may portray one as resilient, understanding, and bold. Think of two lovers or sibling quarreling, but each remains in the established personal space. The message that is being communicated is that the individual is confident that he or she can handle the intense emotions from the other person. For most people, they only allow their lover to stay in their personal distance when feeling upset because they trust that the person can handle the known behavior of the affected person. Since being in a personal space places a person within physical striking range, most people will only allow trusted and familiar individuals into their personal space.

Equally important is that invasion of personal space is justified because it is a part of professional demands. Think of a new teacher that is trying to help a student solve a mathematical equation. In this aspect, the teacher is a stranger because he or she is new to the school. By sitting or standing close to the student, the teacher is invading the personal space, but the established norms in this context allow the student not to feel unease. For emphasis, this case is not unique as it aligns with stated expectations that people will welcome known or unfamiliar people in their personal space only if they trust them and, in this case, the student feels safe with any teacher. For this reason, the operationalization of distance in communication is mediated and moderated by established culture.

In most cases, one can start with public distance before allowing the interaction to happen in a personal or social space. For instance, as a student during tournaments, you could have initiated non-verbal communication with the student from the other college before suddenly feeling connected to the individual and allowing him or her to move into personal space as a potential girlfriend or boyfriend. At first, the target person saw you as a stranger but allowed you to make non-verbal communication within the public space. When the person felt the need to connect more with you and have given you the benefit of the doubt, the person allowed you to move through public distance and social distance to enter their personal space.

For instance, a lot can be learned from studying distance and space in communication. Being allowed into the social and personal distances implies that the person trusts that you will not harm them emotionally and physically. For the intimate distance, being allowed into this distance implies that the person trusts you so much and is confident that you can never harm them and that you share a lot. For instance, a mother holding her baby close enough to her signals that the baby is feeling assured of security and protection. When two lovers move closer until their faces are almost touching suggests trust and confidence that the other person feels safe and protected.

Relatedly, if arguing with your child or lover and the individual moves farther from you physically, then it suggests that the person no longer feels safe with you being within their personal distance. Issues that can cause someone to expand the distance between you and them include the risk of violence from you and emotional issues. If you occasionally act violently, then chances are, your lover or children will expand the personal distance to social distance because this is where they feel safe due to your personality and character. It then appears that your prior behavior will also affect the distance during communication.

Nevertheless, they are other issues that cause individuals to extend the distance of interaction, and these include having a medical condition or having hygiene issues. For instance, if you are sweaty, then chances are that the other person may prefer to extend the distance of communication between you and them. Having oral hygiene issues may also make the other person move far away from you because the smell turns them off. For this reason, interpreting the distance between communicators should also include hygiene and health-related issues that impact this distance.

For instance, some medical conditions can make people maintain some distance from you or be closer to you physically. For instance, some conditions may attract uneasiness, and this includes epilepsy. People with epilepsy get seizures, and this can make people feel unease being closer to them because they inadvertently fall. On the other hand, having hearing issues or sore throat may make people move closer to you physically to facilitate effective communication. However, these are exceptions when analyzing space and distance as forms of non-verbal communication, but they should be taken into account where necessary.

In some cases, it is welcome to invade personal distance merely by the circumstances. For instance, when attending a match in a full packed stadium or sitting to watch a movie in a movie theater, one will have his personal invaded due to the sitting arrangements. In this context, one may feel uneasy with this arrangement, but he or she has little control over the situation. While we value and seek to protect personal spaces, some situations make us allowing the invasion of this space because it is beyond control.

Conclusion

Human behaviors constitute the set of psychic reactions of people, allowing them to preserve relationships with the environment, maintain the phenomenon of life, and ensure its continuity. It is the way of being of the individual and the set of actions that he carries out to adapt himself to an environment. It is the response to motivation, translating motivation as everything that drives an individual to perform a behavior.

The behavior of the individual, when considered in a given space and time, is known as behavior.

Behavior has been the center of the study of psychology since its inception. John B. Watson, a representative of the psychology of behavior or behaviorism, postulated that psychology, instead of being based on introspection, should limit its study to the observation of the individual in a given situation.

The study of behavior investigates the evolution of certain formative stages in the individual, such as childhood or adolescence, and is linked to the study of physical development from birth to death.

Most psychologists today agree that the object of the psychological sciences is human behavior. But, by "human behavior" we understand many things, besides being able to be focused from very diverse points of view. It is the struggle for the life of the premature newborn.

Artists, scientists, teachers, politicians, prepare human behavior when they apply their knowledge and skills to their corresponding tasks.

Human behavior is the fantasies of a child, the dreams of the adolescent, the hallucinations of the alcoholic.

This is well known but little understood.

When we speak of behavior, we point first to the clear and evident activities observable by others: their walking, talking, testicular, their daily activity... this behavior is called evident behavior because it is externally observable.

We can conclude that behavior is the voluntary and involuntary actions that we human beings perform.

www.ingramcontent.com/pod-product-compliance
Lightning Source LLC
Chambersburg PA
CBHW062150100526
44589CB00014B/1772